Never say BOO TO A GHOST

and Other Haunting Rhymes

Chosen by John Foster
Illustrated by Korky Paul

Oxford University Press

OXFORD
UNIVERSITY PRESS

Great Clarendon Street, Oxford OX2 6DP

Oxford University Press is a department of the University of Oxford.
It furthers the University's objective of excellence in research, scholarship,
and education by publishing worldwide in

Oxford   New York

Auckland   Cape Town   Dar es Salaam   Hong Kong   Karachi
Kuala Lumpur   Madrid   Melbourne   Mexico City   Nairobi
New Delhi   Shanghai   Taipei   Toronto

With offices in

Argentina   Austria   Brazil   Chile   Czech Republic   France   Greece
Guatemala   Hungary   Italy   Japan   Poland   Portugal   Singapore
South Korea   Switzerland   Thailand   Turkey   Ukraine   Vietnam

Oxford is a registered trade mark of Oxford University Press
in the UK and in certain other countries

This selection and arrangement © John Foster 1990
Illustrations © Korky Paul 1990

First published 1990

British Library Cataloguing in Publication Data available

ISBN 978-0-19-276310-5

5 7 9 10 8 6 4

Typeset by Pentacor PLC, High Wycombe, Bucks.0

Printed in Great Britain by
CPI Cox & Wyman, Reading, RG1 8EX

Paper used in the production of this book is a natural,
recyclable product made from wood grown in sustainable forests.
The manufacturing process conforms to the environmental
regulations of the country of origin.

For Suzie: K.P.

www.korkypaul.com

Contents

The Ghoul

My head is like a vulture's head;
my skin is cracked like dried-up mud.
For I am of the living dead
and feast on human flesh and blood.

I drag the strangled bodies in
the ruined walls engulfed by mist.
I crunch their bones: my green eyes grin
and blood drips as my thin lips twist.

My fingernails are cracked and black,
my flesh a sickly shade of white,
I lurk round ready to attack
in graveyards at the dead of night.

But please consider this small factor
before you scream or faint with fright:
I'm just a horror movie actor
(it's fish and chips for tea tonight).

Charles Thomson

Who's There?

Who's there?
Just an eddy of air
That tickles the trees.
Only the scuff of a cat
As it noses the leaves.

Who's there?
Just a raising of hair
At the back of the neck.
Only a tug on a nerve
That makes the knees knock.

Who's there?
Just the thrill of a stare
Unseen in the dark.
Only the following eyes
That in black corners lurk.

Who's there?
Just the thought that you share
A deserted lane.
Only the fall of footsteps
That stop when you turn.

Who's there?
Just the creak of a stair
As the storm shakes the house.
Only the tap of a shutter
The wind has worked loose.

Who's there?
Just a wing and a prayer
That you'll pass the night safe.
Only the tingle of terror
From imagination run rife.

Ray Mather

The Zombie Horror

One dark and wintry evening
When snow swirled through the air
And the wind howled like a banshee
I crept silently up the stair.

I sat in the quiet of my bedroom
And opened with baited breath
My Zombie-Horror Make-Up Kit
That would frighten my sister to death.

FRIGHTEN YOUR FAMILY! AMAZE YOUR
    FRIENDS!
WITH OUR DO-IT-YOURSELF MAKE-UP KITS.
BE A WEREWOLF! A VAMPIRE! A ZOMBIE-GHOUL!
SCARE YOUR NEIGHBOURS OUT OF THEIR WITS!

Slowly my face began to change
As I carefully applied the pack.
I grinned at my face in the mirror
But an evil stranger leered back.

Long hair sprouted wild from my forehead,
My nose was half snout, half beak,
My right eye bulged angry and bloodshot
While my left one crawled over my cheek.

My fangs hung long and broken,
My chin was broken with sores,
The backs of my hands were mats of hair
My fingers grew long, bird-like claws.

I heard my sister opening the door,
Heard her call, 'Hello, anyone in?'
I took a long, last look at the thing in the glass
Distorted and ugly as sin.

My sister was running the water
I could hear her washing her hair.
I heard her call out as a floorboard creaked.
'Hello, is that somebody there?'

I released my zombie howl
As I crashed through the kitchen door,
Then I saw this ghoul in the window pane
And passed out cold on the floor.

Gareth Owen

Voice in the Night

I listen, listen
as I lie in bed.

should I pull the covers
over my head?

if I do
then I won't
be able to hear
what it is
that's creeping
near
and nearer
to the house

a ghostly horror
in the night
slithering
slodging
right
beneath my window

but if I don't
hide safe
beneath the sheet
then I'll see it
slothering
over the street

come gaping
in my room
with a ghastly grin

ghoulish-white
gaunt and thin
eyes gleaming red
as bloody pools
glaring inside
black mouth wide
a moor-bleak cave
sharp fangs raise
it's wanting to
hoping to
ready to
taste my blood

I shiver alone
scream silently
wonder why
the vampire
has chosen me

take my fingers
from my ears
as hot tears rise
slide down my cheeks

and hear
a voice outside
crying
out of the darkness
soft
and urgently
'Let me in, our kid!
I've lost my key!'

Joan Poulson

Candy and the Video

Candy spends all night watching video cartoons—wide-eyed ghouls and phantoms chasing shadows round the room, hurtling towards her at freakspeed fastforward, till she traps them in a shivering freezeframe then rewinds them back, again and again, breakdancing at her fingertips as she jinxes the controls —sliding the black cassettes in and out, out and in through the glistening slot that grins in the middle of the machine.

Her sticky fingers slithering, coated with chocolate, smothered with honey, till too late she realizes this video's more hungry than she is, as it sucks in her knuckles, grips at her wrist, twists her elbow and gobbles her arm, then quick as a slurp of a cold cup of coffee it swallows up all the rest of her body, even the bits that aren't covered with toffee.

Its mouth shuts with a clatter and its green light eyes just flicker, stifling a burp as Candy's puzzled features appear on the screen.

Candy's Mum comes into the room, and Candy waves and bangs the glass, but her Mum ignores her and zig-zags past, attacking the groaning carpet, armed with a vacuum cleaner. 'Where's Candy?—I haven't seen her, she'll be off with her mates again. I'm sick and tired of telling her, she's a real little pain. I'll bet she gets in trouble, but at least she's out of my hair . . .'

And Candy's Mum collapses into a padded threadbare
   chair that billows clouds of dust onto the newly-hoovered
   floor as she smiles absent-mindedly at the antics on the
   screen where her daughter's pulling faces, pulling
   tongues and screaming curses.

'These TV shows get worse and worse. I'd better go find
   Candy before she disappears.'

'Don't do it Mum—I'm here, I'm here!'
Candy's face mouths helplessly, as her mother's hand
   hovers, then swoops like a thirsty vampire towards the
   remote control . . .

Dave Ward

The Television Ghost

I'm the ghost you sometimes see appear on television
  screens.
I start off every morning with a meal of egg and beans,

then shoot off twice as fast as any supersonic jet
to haunt some unsuspecting person's television set,

and when they groan out loud, 'Look—there's a ghost all
  round that figure,'
I put my hand up to my mouth and have a good old
  snigger.

They frown, 'The aerial's in the spot it worked well
  yesterday,'
but though they twist it round and round I still don't go
  away.

I wait until they've got it in a very awkward place
and then I vanish, just to see the look upon their face:

they groan, 'Oh no, I can't stand up here on this chair all
  night,'
(I really wish you could be there—it's such a funny
  sight.)

I don't hang round for ever though, because one day I fear
they'll fetch the TV exorcist they call 'The Engineer'.

Charles Thomson

The Ceefax Family

Last night
As we sat glued to the Set,
Mum, Dad and me;
Terry Wogan reached out
And switched us off.
The whole room disappeared
Into a single small white dot.
Now we're all on Ceefax,
Page 103.

David R. Morgan

Locking Up

A frail old woman lived by herself
    As jittery as a mouse.
When darkness fell she locked all locks
    In her rickety rambling house.

She bolted bolts and hooked all hooks
    (No window left unshut):
She checked and rechecked twenty times
    To be quite certain . . . but

What was that? Close to her ear
    A whisper faint and thin,
No body there, but a phantom voice:
    'Now we're both locked in.'

Ian Serraillier

Tables Turned

The ghost of bold Ned Kelly
came to haunt my Auntie Nellie,
but when it saw her in the light
it was the ghost that got the fright.

Michael Dugan

A Night at the Theatre

Now here's a really spooky tale
To give you palpitations—
Two ghosts went to the theatre
To make their reservations.

They went up to the booking office,
Stood waiting in the line,
And on their turn, made this request:
'Two seats for the phantomime. . . .'

Clive Webster

BOX OFFICE

Promotion

A keen traffic warden named Hector
Was killed by a hit-and-run Rector.
   With evident pride
   Hector sighed as he died:
'This makes me a traffic in-SPECTRE.'

Ian Serraillier

Sir Hector

Sir Hector was a spectre
And he loved a lady ghost;
At midnight he'd collect her
And he'd drive her to the coast.

And there upon the shingle
They would rattle all their bones,
And ocean sounds would mingle
With their melancholy moans.

Colin West

When I was Alive

'When I was alive I was short of cash,'
Said the ghost, as he twitched with a spasm.
'Now that I'm dead I'm no better off,
'Cause I'm short of ectoplasm.'

Finola Akister

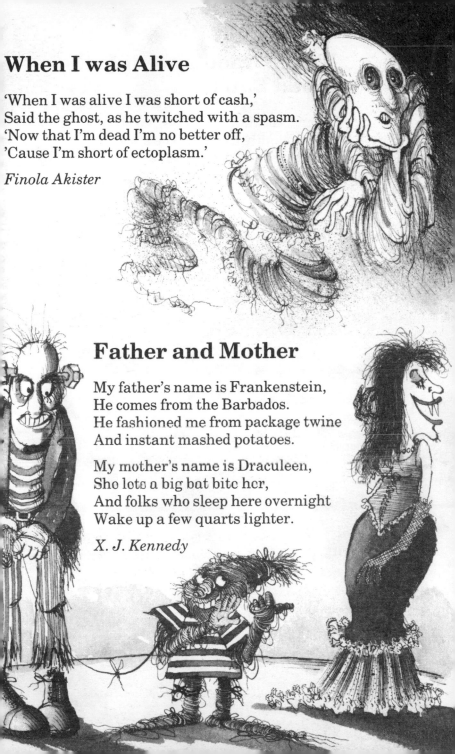

Father and Mother

My father's name is Frankenstein,
He comes from the Barbados.
He fashioned me from package twine
And instant mashed potatoes.

My mother's name is Draculeen,
She lets a big bat bite her,
And folks who sleep here overnight
Wake up a few quarts lighter.

X. J. Kennedy

When Dracula went to the Blood Bank

When Dracula went to the blood bank,
he thoroughly flustered the staff,
for rather than make a donation,
he drew out a pint and a half.

Jack Prelutsky

Lies Again

And then another little boy
Confided to his mummy,
'They say at school that I'm a vampire
And it isn't very funny!'

'Of course it isn't,' Mummy said,
To her darling little tot,
'Now drink your soup up quickly, dear
Or else it's going to clot.'

Clive Webster

High Spirits

A Vampire who lived wholly on yeast,
Said, 'Though all shall one day be deceased,
    It's exceedingly plain
    We will all rise again,
So I'd like to get started at least!'

David R. Morgan

When Dracula went to the Dentist

When Dracula went to the dentist,
The dentist smiled and said,
'There is nothing wrong with your teeth
Except for these specks of red.'

'I wish that I had teeth like yours,'
Said the dentist, brushing away.
'They're the finest set of teeth
I've seen for many a day.'

'You too can have a set like mine,'
Smiled Dracula. 'Here's my cheque.
Just pay it in at the blood bank
Along with that blood from your neck!'

John Foster

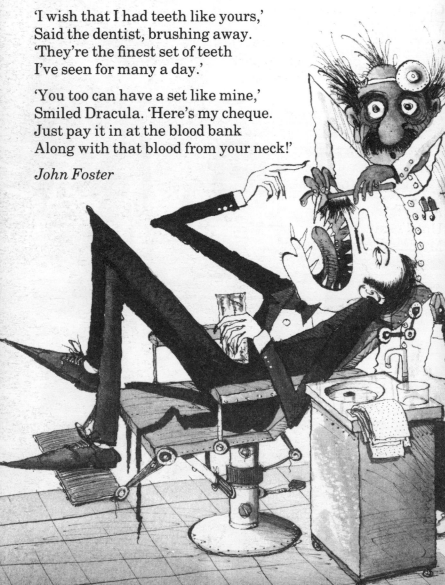

Dracula's Return

After reading
Dracula all evening
It isn't easy believing
The Count's in his coffin.
Going up the stairs to bed
When all is quiet as the dead
And the night is starless and black
What a shock to feel pulled back.
Struggling, you feel the hold
Tighten twofold
And grip you tighter yet
At every step.
You fully expect
To feel next
The fangs in your neck.

A terrible hassle
Until I saw
My dressing-gown tassel
Had caught in the door.

Stanley Cook

Blood Brothers

Jim Dracula and Albert Frankenstein
live on a council estate near Crewe.
The two work on the night shift,
and often travel in together on the bus.
Jim carries his blood sandwiches
in a blue plastic lunchbox, and Albert
always has a flask of steaming, bright green liquid.
Jim runs a one-man transfusion service;
Albert works on the assembly-line
in a body factory.

'I've always been clever with my hands,'
says Albert.
'It's a matter of taste, I suppose,'
says Jim,
licking his lips.

Jim Dracula and Albert Frankenstein
like to roam but are happiest at home
with their work, and can't wait to get back.
Jim has packed his wooden stake and bit of Cheshire soil
in a brand new vinyl coffin,
ready for his package-tour of Transylvania.
Albert has dozed off
while reading his manual of spare-part surgery
in a laboratory high in the mountains.

Jim Dracula and Albert Frankenstein
will be back to the old routine next week,
off to work as the sun sets,
and tucked up in the vault by breakfast-time;
down to the graveyard for fresh supplies,
or fluttering up the front of tower-blocks.

'I haven't had a bite all day,'
says Jim.
'Give us a hand,'
says Albert,
'This one's got one foot
in the grave.'

Adrian Henri

The Vampire's Wedding

For weeks and weeks the town was dreading
the Vampire and the Werewolf's wedding.
The presents were extremely strange—
tooth files and cures for lice and mange,
some rare and vintage blood in vats
and tubs of sugared flies (for bats).

The marriage went off very well.
The vicar flew direct from hell:
he wished them years of endless strife
and then pronounced them bat and wife.
The guests applauded when he sighed,
romantically, 'Now bite the bride!'

According to the best bat's brother,
the new wife ate the bridegroom's mother,
whose husband squeaked, 'I don't mind that—
she always was a daft old bat.'
Beneath the floodlight of the moon
the Death March played (their favourite tune).

Then with a friendly parting curse
they left the party in a hearse,
tossed out a hellebore bouquet
to little ghouls who lined the way,
and honeymooned with loving mania
for several years in Transylvania.

Marian Swinger/Charles Thomson

Small Ads

♥ ——————————— ♥
Headless **giant** (5' 10"tall) seeks **attractive giantess** **(over 20 stone)** view to marriage and setting up **charm school.** P.O.Box 735 Throttlewaite.
♥ ——————————— ♥

Gothic manor *for sale.* *Extensive dungeons with built-in* **torture chamber.** Potential for **expansion.** Needs some modernization. Phone Flogborough 8271 after midnight.

Wanted by animal lover: *Bats, newts, frogs and toads.* 🦇 🦇 🦇 🦇 🦇 Also **large cauldron.** Will collect. Phone Uggleton 381.

Easy-going Ogre seeks 🏠 *lodgings.* Good cook, *fond of young children.* ☎ Phone Grimbleton 9967.

Shy monster, *fond of* **underwater swimming,** Harry Lauder, Haggis, *seeks* **like-minded monsters** • • • • • • • • • • • • • • • • for companionship in *secluded Highland retreat.* Apply Loch Ness.

Lost: One *SCRAWNY* **black cat.** Answers to the name of **Igor**. Left ear missing, vile nature, vicious snarl. Much missed, **reward offered** *for safe return.* Cobweb Cottage, Hobble-on-the-Hill. 🐈

Young-at-heart ghost

(aged 310) seeks lady ghost (aged 280-300) for romantic graveyard walks and chain-rattling sessions. Apply Cobblestone Castle, Sloppington-on-sea.

House-trained dragons for sale. Make excellent children's pets. All colours. Also ideal as alternative central heating. ☏ *Phone Mumblethorpe 6767.*

Reliable phantom seeks night work in or around Highgate. Frightening unwelcome guests a speciality. Enquire Cemetery Gates.

Wanted: **One hundred vampires** *for market research by large False Teeth Factory. Send details of fangs to Head Office, Toothypeg Ltd., Tooting Bec. No personal callers.*

For sale: **one broomstick.** hardly used. Will consider exchange for lady's bicycle. Phone Skipwick 969.

Transylvania in Spring? Send large S.A.E for details of our luxury coach tours. *Special rates for persons of rare blood groups.* Transyl Travel, ☏ London E17.

*Please mention the **Ghoulish Gazette** when answering any of the above ads. Why not place a regular order with your local newsagent?*

Colin West

There Once was a Headless Horseman

It wasn't easy being headless.
Let me tell you, for a start,
I kept falling off my horse.

Not to mention getting lost
and arriving at the crossroads
far too late for frightening
people wandering home at night.

As I galloped through the moonlight,
my pale cloak stretched out behind me,
my sword gleaming through the gloom.

It's hard to snore with no head,
hard to scratch your nose.
It's hard to think with no head
how to see your toes.
It's hard to nod with no head.
In fact, I suppose,
With no head you lose your thread
and your confusion grows.

Then suddenly, three weeks ago
disaster struck, a tragedy
occurred of great proportions.

After several hundred years
of empty space above the neck
and nothing much between the ears,
I woke to find I'd grown a head!

Another one! With two cross eyes,
a broken nose and missing teeth
and scarcely any brain at all.

It's hard to scare folks with a head,
hard to be a ghost.
It's hard to frighten with a head,
hard to make the most
of being headless because a head
denies young ghostly boast.
In fact a head, it could be said,
Is not a thing I need.
It makes a headless horseman feel
Very daft indeed.

David Harmer

Incurable

He was very polite,
removing his head
as I entered the room.
Carefully he placed it
on the coffee table
to stare at my knee-caps.
Having lost it once
on the Queen's orders
he took pains to keep it
always in view.

He had hopes of some
permanent repair job,
what with modern surgery,
or today's instant glue.

His ideas were big
but on examining the head
I saw there was nothing in it.
His punishment had been just
and I saw through him
and his little game.
'Not a ghost of a chance,'
I said.

John C. Desmond

Home Haircut

Nellie, cutting Johnnie's hair,
Was taking insufficient care;
She turned to hear what someone said,
And found that she'd cut off his head!
She smiled, 'I know just what to do,'
And stuck it on again with glue.

John Cunliffe

You'd Forget Your Head . . .

One day I actually did: forgot to screw it on,
Left it on the bedside table—
Easily done.
It certainly simplified the morning wash—
Not the usual rigmarole;
And breakfast? Suppose I must have
Spooned my cornflakes
Into the available hole.
Realized then I was headless
But just thought, 'What the heck!'
Set off for school with my bobble hat
Perched on top of my neck.
Course, the teachers didn't notice:
Too busy splashing red
To notice a simple thing
Like a boy with a missing head.
Chalky called me an idiot,
Wondered where my brains had gone,
'You need to use your head, my lad.'
Well, I would if I'd got it on.

The kids all reckoned it was brilliant, though—
When I took my hat off they roared.
They're all coming like it one day next week,
Chanting, 'We are the Headless Horde!'
Got home: Mum said, 'Do you realize
You went without your head?
Gave me quite a turn
When I went in your room
And found it by your bed.
Mind you, I'm not complaining—
Though it gave a scare to the cat too—
'Cos while I was doing the cleaning
It gave me someone to chat to.'

Eric Finney

Innocence

Sitting down at tea one day
With furrowed-brow expression,
Young Jimmy asked his Mummy dear
A most perplexing question.

'Mummy dear, can you help me—
It's something I've just read,
About a nasty werewolf—
What's one of those?' he said.

His Mummy dear looked at her son,
With loving, kindly eye.
'Don't ask questions, just comb your face,'
Was her tender, sweet reply.

Clive Webster

A Wolf is at the Laundromat

A wolf is at the Laundromat,
it's not a wary stare-wolf,
it's short and fat, it tips its hat,
unlike a scary glare-wolf.

It combs its hair, it clips its toes,
it is a fairly rare wolf,
that's only there to clean its clothes—
it is a wash-and-wear-wolf.

Jack Prelutsky

Full Moon

At times of full moon
(I wish I knew why)
I get a strange yearning
to howl at the sky!

For reasons peculiar
I've not yet discovered,
the backs of my hands then
with fur become covered!

My fingernails lengthen,
my feet look like paws!
I feel a compulsion
to walk on all fours!

My eyes redly glimmer,
hair sprouts from my ears.
Fang-like my teeth grow,
with points sharp as spears!

Though normally fussy
about what I eat,
on nights when the moon's full,
I crave *raw red meat!*

Robin Klein

A Good Hiding

Why are we hiding in here, mother,
Why are we hiding in here?
What monsters are coming, what men in black
What grim-clad figures on the attack?
Why are we hiding in here?

Why are we hiding in here?
Tell me the truth, mum, please.
Is it the taxman?
Is it the axeman?
Is it the secret police?

Why are we hiding in here, mother,
Give me an answer, please.
Is it a giant slug?
Is it a doodlebug?
Is it that runny cheese?

There's nothing at all to fear, dear,
Nothing at all to fear.
It's just Aunt Gladys and Uncle Jim:
If we keep really quiet they won't know we're in:
That's why we're hiding in here, dear,
That's why we're hiding in here.

Trevor Millum

Horror Story

'There are no such things as ghosts,'
he said,
As he locked himself in the haunted room.
He's been in there for fifty years.
I wonder if he'll come out soon?

Adam Coleman

The Cupboard On The Landing

Mary had been told
Never to wipe her nose on her skirt,
Never to run in the house,
And
Never never to open the cupboard on the landing.

But one day,
After blowing her nose on a clean handkerchief,
She walked up the stairs,
Intent upon opening the cupboard on the landing.

First she
Turned the key in the lock,
Then she turned the other key in the other lock,
Slid back the top bolt,
The bottom bolt
And the six bolts in between.
Then she cut through the chains,
Removed the barbed wire,
Switched off the alarm,
Threw her handkerchief over the video camera,
Undid the combination
And opened the cupboard door.

And what did Mary see
In the cupboard on the landing?
Nothing.
But
Something in the cupboard on the landing saw Mary.
And Mary was never seen again.

John Coldwell

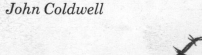

Ghost Hunt

Long after midnight
I searched for the haunted house,
(ooooohhhhh)
but I didn't see
    a speck of a spectre
    nor a fraction of a phantom
    nor a spot of a spook
    nor a pinch of a poltergeist.

I didn't even catch the sweet scent
of a skelington's wellingtons!

Long after midnight
I searched for the haunted house,
(ooooohhhhh)
but when I couldn't find it
—I gave up the ghost.

John Rice

The Haunting

At the foot of the bed in the dead of the night
  It stood there, or rather it *hovered*—
Two luminous eyes and a face ghastly white
  From which I have never recovered.

When I asked, 'Who are you?' It looked taken aback,
  Indeed, you could say It looked frightened;
But then, *I* was too, and my hair, raven-black,
  From that moment has curiously whitened.

So I asked It once more, 'Who *are* you?'—Again
  Its pale lips moved mockingly, mutely,
While the night-wind howled loud in the sobbing rain
  And It stared back, trembling acutely.

Which seeing, I screwed up my courage and switched
  On the lamp, hands fumbling in terror—
Then my eyes met a jibbering idiot who twitched
  Like my twin in the newly hung mirror.

Raymond Wilson

The Diary

THURSDAY OCTOBER 28TH	Ghastlyfright Hall, Much Haunting-on-the-Wolds. 7.15 p.m. I don't believe all this stuff about ghosts, So, to prove it once and for all, I've decided to spend five days all alone Here, at Ghastlyfright Hall! 10.00 p.m. It's now 10.00 p.m. and there's nothing about, I've not even heard a chain rattle. Huh, all this talk of spectres and spooks – I'll soon put an end to their prattle!
FRIDAY OCTOBER 29TH	9.00 p.m. Well, another day draws near to its close And still no apparition! It just goes to prove what I thought all along: It's only daft superstition. Still, only another three days to go Then I can collect my bet. Five hundred pounds to stay in this house? No wonder the owner's in debt!
SATURDAY OCTOBER 30TH	10.15 a.m. There appears to be a change in the weather, The Hall feels colder today. I've lit a large fire in my bedroom So I'll be warm there, anyway. 9.45 p.m. A strange thing happened this evening: And I just don't know who to blame, As I turned off the lights downstairs I'm sure someone whispered my name!
SUNDAY OCTOBER 31ST	9.30 a.m. I think I know what happened last night, It wasn't some ghostly uttering! I was a little overtired, that's all; It was only the wind in the guttering. Even so, I don't feel relaxed, I can feel eyes unseen, And it is with growing dismay That I've noticed tonight's Hallowe'en!

11.45 p.m.
It's a quarter to twelve and I'm terrified!
A thunderstorm rages without.
A fork of lightning has hit the roof
And all the lights have gone out!
12.00 a.m.
The clock has struck twelve! It's the witching hour!
But I am n-not one that easily sc-scares,
So I'm sure it's just rats in the rafters
And not footsteps on the stairs!
Ssh! Listen again! They're coming this way!
AAAGH!! There's a hand on the door!!
NO! NO! PLEASE LEAVE ME ALONE!
I DON'T THINK I CAN TAKE ANY MORE...

Much Haunting-on-the-Wolds General Hospital

**MONDAY
NOVEMBER 1ST**

11.15 a.m.
I should be touched to receive these flowers,
I was brought up to be forgiving,
But after that stupid prank last night
I'm lucky to still be living!
I leapt out of the window and onto the lawn,
Broke a leg, an arm and two fingers,
Just to find it was only a joke,
I'd been scared by two trick-or-treaters!

Ray Mather

A Go'st Story!

Sir,
   It hath been a source of some regret
That thou should'st not have seen me yet.
Dost thou realize ye anguish and pain
Thou causeth me when thou hear'st not my chain
As it rattleth and scrapeth at stroke of midnight?
Gadzooks, man, it's meant to give thee a fright!
Thou always sleep soundly alone in thy bed
From whence, for centuries, all others hath fled.
I prideth myself on my dread apparition
But thou, alas, abjure superstition!
Now at ghostly reunions I'm made laughing-stock
Because I'm unable to give thee a shock.
I've exhausteth ye usual haunted house tricks;
Sent icy draughts, snuff'd candle-wicks,
Made ye door-keys flyeth across ye floor,
But discourteous youth, thou continu'st to snore!
I'm sorely vexed, I've nothing left,
Of all good-will I'm totally bereft.
I know'st ye fault lieth only with thee,
Researchers cam'st here from afar to hunt me,
So, I serv'st thee notice, tomorrow I quit.
My white sheet is pack'd for ye moonlight flit.
I go'st to a house where I knowst I shall merit—
For ye owners there know how to join in ye spirit!

Yours ethereally,
Ye Ghoste

Ray Mather

Walls I Scream

When I went to the Grange for the Ball
And nervously stood in the hall,
I asked of my host,
'Is there maybe a ghost?'
He said 'Nope,' turned, and walked through the wall.

The butler stood straight, pale and tall
And said in half moan and half drawl,
'Hat and coat, if you please,'
Then with consummate ease
He took them away through the wall.

'Well hello there,' I heard a voice call.
For her beauty I'd certainly fall.
Her eyes were beguiling,
Her sweet lips still smiling
As *she* disappeared through the wall.

My knees knocked. I feared I would fall.
My skin was beginning to crawl,
Couldn't stand any more
So I rushed for the door
That at least would get *me* through the wall.

'Though her charms would for ever enthrall
I dared not go back there at all.
Then with heart full of terror
I made the grave error
Of driving my car through a wall.

Now I'm also a ghost at the Hall
So why don't you give us a call?
'Though the thought might well daunt you
We'd be delighted to haunt you
And then drive you right up the wall.

Philip C. Gross

Fantasy Fighter

I've diced with death a thousand times
and lived to tell the tale.
I've wrestled a dozen lions,
faced sharks and a killer whale.

I've fought with the sword of the Samurai
till the dragons turned and fled.
I've wielded a two-bladed axe
and scythed a hydra's head.

Medusa and the Minotaur,
thought they had me beat
till I threw a six and scorched them
with a beam of laser heat.

In the cave of one-eyed Cyclops
the floor was strewn with bones,
I waited till he shambled in
then split his eye with stones.

I zapped the invisible furies,
warned off goblins with just one look.
I gave a space demon such a clout
that I knocked him out of the book.

But the moment I close my eyes
there's no chance of escaping attack.
Sleep bids my enemies enter
and nothing can hold them back.

Brian Moses

A 'Humerus' Tale

The skeletons put on a show,
danced round the churchyard in a row,
told jokes and sang a jolly tune
beneath the spotlight of the moon—

except for one who sat alone
and wailed, 'I've lost my funnybone.
It must have fallen from my pocket.'
(At this a tear rolled out each socket.)

At dawn they sank into the ground.
Their cackles died to leave the sound,
beside the little church at Fobbing,
of one sole skeleton's sad sobbing.

But where he'd thrown himself to weep
upon the graveyard rubbish heap,
he saw behind a broken stone
and half a vase—a funnybone.

He quickly pushed it in his vest
and pranced away to join the rest.
Next moment from the rubbish heap
a bony voice began to weep . . .

Marian Swinger/Charles Thomson

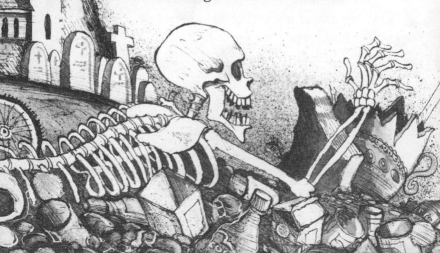

Bill Bones

Bill Bones came home
And he wanted his tea
So he let himself in
With a skeleton key.

Ian Larmont

R.I.P.

'Who's that coughin' in the coffin
In the grave that's next to me?'
Asked the skeleton awoken
As the clock struck half past three.

'At this unearthly hour
I resent a noisy pest.
How can self-respecting bodies
Give their weary bones a rest?'

Wendy P. Larmont

Never Say Boo to a Ghost!

It's a big day for junior ghost—
It's his practical Haunting Test.
Theory was easy as pie—
Passed with merit, ahead of the rest.
He's a pretty scholarly chap,
Knows his Nightway Code to perfection.
It's hard to catch him out—
He's clued up on every section.
Knows all there is about haunting
When, where, and how, to appear.
Off he goes, cheerful, elated
Shining L plates at front and rear.
He's literally floating on air
Smug to his last misty particle.
Knows he's Grade One ghost of the year
He's quite the genuine article.

Daylight, and now he's returned;
But what has become of his poise?
Gone is the confident air
He's emitting a pitiful noise . . .
He carefully followed the book—
Wailing and groans in the night—
And how did his victims behave?
Did they scatter and hide in their fright?
Not a bit. They smiled in contempt;
Replied to his groans with a 'Boo!'
And completely destroyed his aplomb
With 'Don't think that WE'RE scared of YOU!'
Now he'll never be haunting again—
The junior ghost's in disgrace.
After all, you can't do with a ghost
Too frightened to show his own face!

Margaret Porter

Uncle George and the Gees

Uncle George woke up one morning
                    with a very strange disease.
He found he could only do things
                    that began with letter 'G's.
He could goggle and gurgle and gargle,
                    gawp and grin and grunt.
He could gallop and gollop and gossip,
                    and glue things back to front.
He could gamble, and gambol up gangways,
                    or dance an old-fashioned
                    gavotte.
But he couldn't boil his kettle
                    or put the tea in the pot.
His cornflakes tasted gritty;
                    gravy gushed over his toast.
He ate golden syrup and gingernuts,
                    and couldn't read his post.
He wrapped himself in a groundsheet—
                    he couldn't wear his suit—
He put on his gloves and galoshes.
                    His wife said, 'You look cute.'
He gave his guinea-pigs groundsel
                    and cleaned his garden gnomes.
But his hair was a mess because
                    he couldn't use brushes or combs.

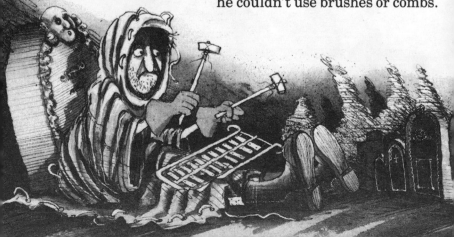

He couldn't drive to the office,
                    or catch a train or a bus.
So he grovelled there with a gorilla
                    from the London Zoo called Gus.
He couldn't sit down in his office.
                    He glided into the gym,
Giving orders that gadgets and grievances
                    should be brought there to him.
His secretary said, 'Mr Grant
                    dictates with such perfect
                    grammar.
I know he gabbles and gibbers,
                    but at least he doesn't stammer.'
When the others went out to lunch
                    George gobbled grilled gammon
                    and Guinness.
He had to refuse when prim Mrs Dews
                    said, 'Innyone for tinnis,'
'Cos he couldn't play tennis or cricket or squash,
                    and certainly not football.
All he could do was bowl googlies
                    against the garden wall.
Poor George became grizzled and grumpy;
                    he started gnawing his gnails;
Especially now as the weather
                    seemed to be nothing but gales.
They'd find him grieving in graveyards
                    playing Gluck on his
                    glockenspiel.
Even the gargoyles guffawed:
                    'The guy's got no feel.'

But on a grand, golden evening,
>>while goats were grazing the
>>grass,
A girl-guide, giggling gushingly,
>>gave George a glittering glass
Of gooseberry and grape juice.
>>'Drink it,' she said, and grinned.
Glug, glug! Ooh! George felt giddy.
>>He groaned. A gigantic wind
Blew him into a grimy grotto,
>>greasy, grey-green, grotesque,
Where a grisly ghost sat grimacing
>>at a government office desk.
'George,' said the ghost, 'here's a riddle,
>>which you are obliged to guess.
If you guess right, why, yes, tonight
>>you'll be cured of your G-
>>sickness.
So tell me the meaning of this song
When I sound the gong:

Dong:

'Auntie's butter cookies do easily fry.
Happy Indian junior kings
Love munching naughtily orange pie.
Quickly Robin sings
To Uncle Victor whose eXercise
Yanks zither-strings.'

Then George said 'Gosh!' and 'Golly!' and 'Gee!'
'It's tosh,
But it's jolly,
And I'm free!
'Cos not one word
Of your riddle rhyme
Begins with the letter 'G'.'

Uncle George taught all of us
        the riddle of the grey-green
        ghost,
In case we should come down to breakfast,
        and find grey globules of
        glutinous, gungy gruel,
        instead of cornflakes,
        marmalade, and toast.
So please keep Uncle George happy by saying after me
The riddle which set him free:

'Auntie's Butter Cookies Do Easily Fry.
Happy Indian Junior Kings
Love Munching Naughtily Orange Pie.
Quickly Robin Sings
To Uncle Victor Whose eXercise
Yanks Zither-strings.'

Leo Aylen

Ghostly Lessons

Ma, I want some chocolate,
just *one* little treat—
peppermint or strawberry cream . . .

GHOSTS DON'T EAT!

Ma, I've got a toothache,
a pain beneath my heel;
my throat's too sore to work tonight . . .

GHOSTS DON'T FEEL!

Ma, I really hate the dark—
I hate the way they stared!
I'm scared of graveyards, woods and folk . . .

GHOSTS AREN'T SCARED!

Judith Nicholls

Spell to Make Your Teacher Disappear

From the blackboard gather chalk-dust,
Mix it with a drop of ink,
Put it in an empty paint-pot
Rinsed out at the staff-room sink.

Stir it gently with a ruler,
Let it bubble till it's thick.
Make a pair of magic passes
O'er it with a metre stick.

Gently chant the eight times table
Backwards down to eight times one;
Leave it now to gather power—
Soon the magic will be done.

As the hometime bell is ringing
Cringe and wait in fright and fear:
Watch your teacher put her coat on . . .
Watch!—and soon she'll disappear!

S. J. Saunders

Flonster Poem

the flime devoured the floober
and the flummie dined on flime
the fleemie gulped the flummie down
in scarcely any time

the fleener chewed the fleemie
but in hardly half a wink
he was swallowed by the floodoo
who was eaten by the flink

the flink was rather careless
and was gobbled to the bone
by an enterprising flibble,
who fell victim to the flone

the floath who fed upon the flone
soon met another floath
and while they wondered what to do
the flakker ate them both

Jack Prelutsky

The Creature in the Classroom

It appeared inside our classroom
at a quarter after ten,
it gobbled up the blackboard,
three erasers and a pen.
It gobbled teacher's apple
and it bopped her with the core.
'How dare you!' she responded.
'You must leave us . . . there's the door.'

The Creature didn't listen
but described an arabesque
as it gobbled all her pencils,
seven notebooks and her desk.
Teacher stated very calmly,
'Sir! You simply cannot stay,
I'll report you to the principal
unless you go away!'

But the thing continued eating,
it ate paper, swallowed ink,
as it gobbled up our homework
I believe I saw it wink.
Teacher finally lost her temper.
'OUT!' she shouted at the creature.
The creature hopped beside her
and GLOPP . . . it swallowed teacher.

Jack Prelutsky

The Ghost of Classroom Three

There's a tapping at the window,
A moaning at the door,
And something ectoplasmic
Sticking to the floor . . .

But don't panic, don't be frightened
By anything you see,
It's really nothing special,
Just the ghost of classroom three.

It doesn't come out often,
Maybe once or twice a year.
It wanders round and mutters,
Then . . . poof! It disappears.

Sometimes it sits at the desk
Marking books continually . . .
But it's really nothing special,
Just the ghost of classroom three.

Some say it was a teacher
Who met a nasty end . . .
She had a class of awful kids
Who drove her round the bend.

And sometimes there is screaming,
And it weeps, dismally . . .
But it's really nothing special,
Just the ghost of classroom three.

She swore she'd come and haunt them,
But they laughed and didn't care,
And now she haunts the cupboard
(Which otherwise is bare).

And sometimes there are others,
A whole classful you can see,
Doing endless homework
For the ghost of classroom three.

Some say it isn't possible,
And that it's just a story . . .
But classroom three, you must admit,
Feels different . . . sort of *eerie*.

And once, upon the blackboard
Someone wrote mysteriously,
'I'll haunt this school for ever . . .
I'm the ghost of classroom three.'

There's a rapping on the desk tops,
There's a rattling at the door,
And something trying to get out
Of teacher's locked desk drawer . . .

But don't panic, don't be frightened,
Don't scare too easily;
It's really nothing special;
Just the ghost of classroom three . . .

Tony Bradman

Packed Lunches . . . at the School for Witches

'What have you brought
for lunch today?'

> *'Caterpillars in sauce.
> What about you?'*

'Some roast mice
wrapped in mouldy hay.'

> *'And I've got a stick
> to chew.'*

'What's your drink?
Mine's . . . . . something blue!'

> *'This litre tin
> of red gloss paint.'*

'Ah! Look, my favourite!
Pigs' kidneys in glue!'

> *'Phew! The smell makes me
> feel quite faint!'*

'Right, let's eat!
This School for Witches
is a spell-binding place!'

> *'I agree,
> and our packed lunches
> are disgustingly ace!'*

Wes Magee

The Trainee Witch

I'm a trainee witch,
my name is Joan
and today I tried
some spells on my own.

I tried to turn a cassette player
    into a cat
but it ended up
    as a cricket bat.

I tried to turn a tractor
    to a killer whale
but it ended up
    as a fingernail.

I tried to turn a lawnmower
    into a toad
but it ended up
    as a hole in the road.

I tried to turn a chimney
    to a fleet of ships
but it ended up
    as a bag of chips.

I tried to turn a television
    into a doll
but it ended up
    as a sausage roll.

I'm a trainee witch,
my name is Joan
but I'm not very good
at spells on my own.

Charles Thomson

The Spell

You're not supposed to give out spells,
But *you* can have just one.
Now promise not to pass it on
To friend or foe—or anyone!

This one's for turning ankles green
To make them glow at night
So that your feet can see to walk
When there isn't any light.

You mince up a toad in the Magimix,
And pickle a cat in wine,
Then you toss in a couple of dandelions
And a spoonful of turpentine . . .

What's wrong with you now?
Why're you looking like that?
You said that you wanted a spell.
I've given you one. It isn't a trick.
You look so peculiar. Oh, please don't be sick.

Michael Glover

Limited

I once knew a witch who
spoke in words of one syllable.
Easy to understand but
only good for a short spell.

John C. Desmond

The Witch's Tooth

The witch had a tooth
Which was left from her youth
And at night, in the dark, it would glow.
One day, with a cough,
The whole tooth snapped right off
And she bit herself right in the toe.

Ian Larmont

Winnie the . . .

Now three young men, all eager and keen
Wanted to get on in the world,
So they paid a visit to an old smelly witch—
She was good at spells, so they'd heard.

In they went and said to the crone,
'Please tell us what we must do—
We want good careers with lots of money
And that's why we've come to see you.'

'That's easy,' she croaked. 'No trouble at all,
I've a spell that'll do just the trick.
Just spend one hour in my dark, dismal cell
And I'll grant you one wish double quick.'

'And the first wish you make is what you will be
So think carefully before you speak.
For when it is done there is no turning back—
Take heed, for my promise I keep.'

So into her cell the first young man went
And a stench hit him full in the face—
Dead cats, rancid food, blocked drains and the like
And manure all over the place.

But holding his nose as tight as he could
He managed to gasp out his wish:
'I want to be a lawyer,' he said
Through the fetid pong of dead fish.

And one hour later, when he came out
In a new pin stripe suit he was dressed,
With a briefcase full of all he would need
To pass every known legal test.

Then in went the second to make his request
And he held his nose tightly as well,
As the horrible stench stopped him dead in his tracks—
He'd never known quite such a smell.

But he, like the first, gasped out his desire:
'A doctor is what I would hope.'
And sure enough when the poor chap came out
He'd a black bag and big stethoscope.

Then in went the third to choose his career,
With the stench still pervading the air.
'I want to be . . . . POOH!' he said, catching a whiff,
And he came out, changed into a bear . . . .

Clive Webster

Wild Witches' Ball

late last night at wildwitchhall
we witches held our wild witch ball.
in every size and shape and weight
we witches came to celebrate.

ten tall crones with moans and groans
battled in barrels with bats and bones.
nine queer dears with pointed ears
dangled and swang from the chandeliers.

witches eight with mangy tresses
danced with seven sorceresses.
witches six in shaggy rags
played toss and tag with five old hags.

four fat bags took healthy bites
from parts of three unsightly frights.
two fierce furies dug a ditch
and tumbled in one lumpy witch.

there were witches squeezed in every nook
whichever where you cared to look.
how many witches can you see
at our annual wildwitch witches' spree?

Jack Prelutsky

My Sad Friend

I knew a witch that couldn't spell.
She lived at the bottom of a garden well.
I used to shout things down to her
(She was right miserable down there)
Like: Why can't you magic yourself up?
It's warm where I live on the top . . .
Because I can't spel SPEL! she'd call.
Her voice was strange, so faint and small.
And if you can't spel SPEL you're lost.
The magic just won't work at all!

Michael Glover

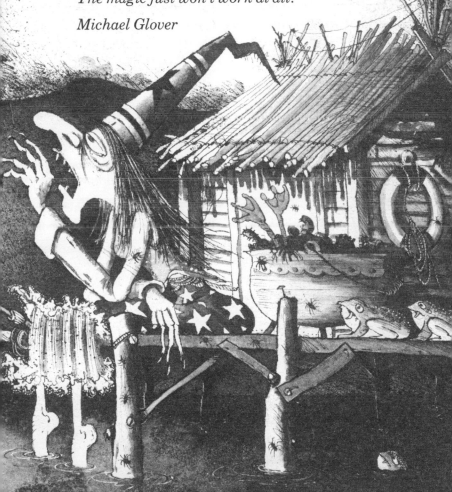

Candy's Camera

Candy's camera takes photographs of things you didn't
know were there.

She took a photo of Auntie Beth, and when the picture
came back from the shop, she had spiders crawling
through her hair.

She took a photo of Uncle Arthur standing by his garden
shed, and when the picture came out, there was a
seagull sitting on his head.

She took some more photos of autumn trees with the first
leaves drifting through the air, but by the time she
went to the shop to collect them, all of the branches in
the pictures were bare.

She took a photo of the corner shop where her mother
went to get bread, but when the pictures came back,
there was a super-market there instead.

She took a photo of her cousin's wedding when the bride
and the groom were kissing, but when the pictures
came back from the shop, one of the bridesmaids was
missing.

Nobody saw her for weeks, nobody knew where she went,
until Candy's camera snapped a photo one day and
there she was arm-in-arm with a gent in the corner
behind Candy's friend Sue, who was chewing a bagful
of toffees. When Candy looked at the photo again, they
were outside the Registry Office. The gent was wearing
his best suit with a carnation in the lapel. Candy's
cousin's bridesmaid liked weddings so much she'd gone
off and got married as well.

Dave Ward

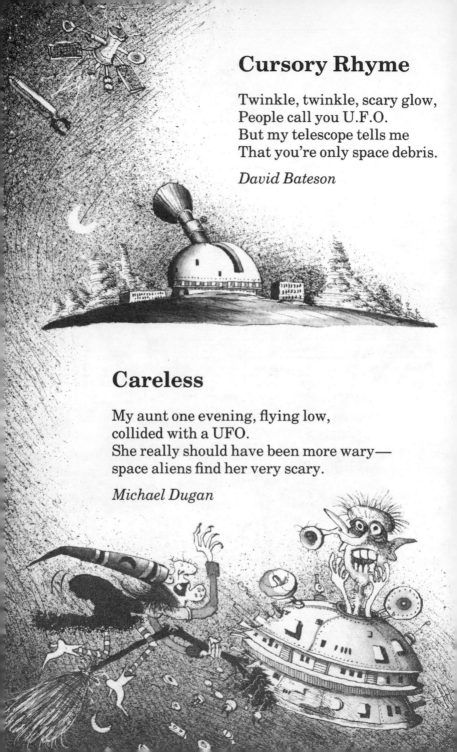

Cursory Rhyme

Twinkle, twinkle, scary glow,
People call you U.F.O.
But my telescope tells me
That you're only space debris.

David Bateson

Careless

My aunt one evening, flying low,
collided with a UFO.
She really should have been more wary—
space aliens find her very scary.

Michael Dugan

Out of a Cloud

I have never seen one,
William saw one though,
He said it hummed like hives of bees
He said it glowed a glow
He said it swooped out of a cloud
And lit the trees below,
He said: 'It took my heart away,'
William's U.F.O.

And ever since that evening,
Wandering here and there,
William scanned the sky each night
With his hopeful stare,
Examining the milky way,
Venus, the Plough, the Bear,
Searching, wishing, longing,
William head-in-air.

And then, one day, he . . . vanished.
How? We'll never know;
We found no clue or trace of him,
Hunting high and low,
Except, spiked on a barbed wire fence,
A note saying: 'Told you so,'
And all around the grass pressed down . . .
Where did William go?

Richard Edwards

The Ghost-cage

The ghost
Made no attempt to struggle,
Allowed us to catch him,
Place him inside the specially designed,
Portable, ghost-cage,
Sat quietly, whatever joltings
He received from the jogged shoulders
Of the native bearers, tripping and stumbling
Over roots or rocks in the mountain gulleys,
Accepted without protest bananas
And platefuls of mealie porridge,
Did not beat his chest,
Did not complain at the bumpy landrover-ride,
Or the less than adequate take-off
Of Charlie's chipped Cessna.
Transferred to a larger cage,
He seemed to be sleeping contentedly
Through most of the twelve-hour jet-flight to London.
'Docile! Utterly docile!'
Was the universal comment
As the moment came for which we had all been waiting
His installation in the quarters
Specially built for him in the London Zoo.
In front of the teevee cameras,
He, for the first time, smiled,
Walked through the supposedly ghost-proof bars
Into the crowd, and vanished.

Leo Aylen

Two's Company

They said the house was haunted, but
He laughed at them and said, 'Tut, tut!
I've never heard such tittle-tattle
As ghosts that groan and chains that rattle;
And just to prove I'm in the right,
Please leave me here to spend the night.'

They winked absurdly, tried to smother
Their ignorant laughter, nudged each other,
And left him just as dusk was falling
With a hunchback moon and screech-owls calling.
Not that this troubled him one bit;
In fact, he was quite glad of it,
Knowing it's every sane man's mission
To contradict all superstition.

But what is that? Outside it seemed
As if chains rattled, someone screamed!
Come, come, it's merely nerves, he's certain
(But just the same, he draws the curtain).
The stroke of twelve—but there's no clock!
He shuts the door and turns the lock
(Of course, he knows that no one's there,
But no harm's done by taking care!)
Someone's outside—the silly joker,
(He may as well pick up the poker!)
That noise again! He checks the doors,
Shutters the windows, makes a pause

To seek the safest place to hide—
(The cupboard's strong—he creeps inside).
'Not that there's anything to fear,'
He tells himself, when at his ear
A voice breathes softly, 'How do you do!
I am the ghost. Pray, who are you?'

Raymond Wilson

If You Come to Our House

If you come to our house
In the middle of the night,
You're sure to get
An awful fright.
It's choc-a-bloc full
Of ghosts, you see,
But whatever they do,
They can't scare me!

There are two little baby ghosts
Playing on the stairs,
And a headless horseman
Saying his prayers;
And a spook in the toilet
Having a pee,
But whatever they do,
They can't scare me!

There's a ghoul in the garden,
Playing with the cat,
And another on the patio,
Wearing granny's hat;
Apparitions in the kitchen,
Having their tea,
But whatever they do,
They can't scare me!

There's a boggart in the chimney
Slowing up the fire,
And a cellar-full of spirits,
All singing in a choir.
There are zombies in the parlour,
Watching TV,
But whatever they do,
They can't scare me!

If you come to our house
In the middle of the night,
You're sure to get
An awful fright.
It's choc-a-bloc full
Of ghosts, you see,
But . . . whatever . . . they . . . do . . . ,
But whatever they . . .
But what . . . !
But . . . !
Aaaaaaaaaaaaarrrrrrrrrggggggghhhhhhh !

John Cunliffe

The Ghost Interview

What do ghosts eat for breakfast?
The smell of burnt toast.

What do ghosts eat for dinner?
The smell of Sunday's roast.

What do ghosts eat for tea?
The smell of the sandwiches that were lost.

What do ghosts wear at knight?
The mail order that was lost in the post.

Where do ghosts live?
Behind the creaking door post.

What do ghosts dream of?
Being alive. That's what they think of most.

Leo Aylen

Horrors

Curse of Count Dracula
Return of the Damned
Revenge of the Werewolf
Mummy Hold my Hand.

Norman Silver

Index of First Lines and Titles

Acknowledgements

The editor and publisher are grateful for permission to include the following copyright material in this anthology.

Finola Akister, 'When I Was Alive', © 1990 Finola Akister. Reprinted by permission of the author. Leo Aylen, 'Uncle George and the Gees', from *Rhymoceros* (Macmillan 1989); 'The Ghost-Cage' and 'The Ghost Interview' both © 1990 Leo Aylen. All reprinted by permission of the author.   David Bateson, 'Cursory Rhyme', © 1990 David Bateson. Reprinted by permission of the author.   Tony Bradman, 'The Ghost of Classroom Three' from *All Together Now* (Viking Kestrel, 1989), © 1989 Tony Bradman. Reprinted by permission of the author and Rogers Coleridge & White Ltd.   John Coldwell, 'The cupboard on the landing' © 1990 John Coldwell. Reprinted by permission of the author.   Adam Coleman, 'Horror Story', © Adam Coleman.   Reprinted by permission of the author.   Stanley Cook, 'Dracula's Return', © 1990 Stanley Cook. Reprinted by permission of the author.   John Cunliffe, 'If You Come To Our House', © 1990 John Cunliffe; 'Home Haircut' from *Standing on a Strawberry* (Deutsch). Both reprinted by permission of David Higham Associates Ltd.   John C Desmond, 'Incurable' and 'Limited', both © 1990 John C Desmond. Reprinted by permission of the author.   Michael Dugan, 'Tables Turned' from *Flocks' Socks and Other Shocks*. Reprinted by permission of Penguin Books Australia Ltd. 'Careless' from *The Worst Dream of All and other Funny Poems* © Michael Dugan 1989. Reproduced with the permission of Harper Collins Australia.   Richard Edwards, 'Out of a Cloud', © 1990 Richard Edwards. Reprinted by permission of the author.   Eric Finney, 'You'd Forget Your Head . . .', © 1990 Eric Finney. Reprinted by permission of the author.   John Foster, 'When Dracula went to the dentist', © 1990 John Foster. Reprinted by permission of the author.   Michael Glover, 'The Spell' and 'My Sad Friend', both © 1990 Michael Glover. Reprinted by permission of the author.   Philip C Gross, 'Walls I Scream', © 1990 Philip C Gross. Reprinted by permission of the author.   David Harmer, 'There was once a headless horseman,' © 1990 David Harmer. Reprinted by permission of the author.   Adrian Henri, 'Blood Brothers', from *The Phantom Lollipop Lady* (Methuen) Reprinted by permission of Rogers Coleridge & White Ltd.   X J Kennedy, 'Father and Mother', from *One Winter Night In August* (Atheneum). copyright © 1975 by X J Kennedy. Reprinted by permission of Curtis Brown Ltd. (New York).   Robin Klein. 'Full Moon' from *Snakes and Ladders*, © Robin Klein 1985. Reprinted by permission of Houghton Mifflin, Australia Pty Ltd., and Oxford University Press.   Ian Larmont, 'Bill Bones', previously published in *Madtail Miniwhale* (Viking/Kestrel, 1989) as 'Old Bill Bones, © 1989 Ian Larmont; 'The Witch's Tooth', © 1990 Ian Larmont. Both reprinted by permission of the author.   Wendy Larmont, 'R.I.P.', © 1990 Wendy Larmont. Reprinted by permission of the author.   Wes Magee, 'Packed lunches . . . at the school for Witches', © 1990 Wes Magee. Reprinted by permission of the author.   Ray Mather, 'Who's there', 'A Go'st Story!' and 'The Diary', all © 1990 Ray Mather. Reprinted by permission of the author.   Trevor Millum, 'A Good Hiding', © 1990 Trevor Millum. Reprinted by permission of the author.   David R Morgan, 'The Ceefax Family', © David R Morgan. Reprinted by permission of the author.   Brian Moses, 'Fantasy Fighter', © 1990 Brian Moses. Reprinted by permission of the author.   Judith Nicholls, 'Ghostly Lessons', © 1990 Judith Nicholls. Reprinted by permission of the author.   Gareth Owen, 'The Ghoul' from *Salford Road*. Reprinted by permission of Rogers Coleridge & White Ltd.   Margaret Porter, 'Never Say Boo to a Ghost!', © Margaret Porter. Reprinted by permission of the author.   Joan Poulson, 'Voice in the Night', © 1990 Joan Poulson. Reprinted by permission of the author.   Jack Prelutsky, 'When Dracula Went to the Blood Bank' and 'A Wolf is at the Laundromat' from *The New Kid on the Block*. Reprinted by permission of Heinemann Young Books. 'Flonster Poem' from *The Snopp on the Sidewalk*, copyright © 1976,77 by Jack Prelutsky; 'The Creature in the Classroom' from *The Baby Uggs are Hatching*, copyright © 1982 by Jack Prelutsky. Reprinted by permission of Greenwillow Books, a division of William Morrow & Co. 'Wild Witches' Ball' from *Witch Poems* (Holiday House, 1976/Pepper Press, 1980). Copyright © 1976 by Jack Prelutsky. Reprinted by permission of the author.   John Rice, 'Ghost Hunt', © 1990 John Rice. Reprinted by permission of the author.   S. J. Saunders, 'Spell to Make Your Teacher Disappear' from *Presenting Poetry 2*, ed. McCall & Palmer. Reprinted by permission of Longman Group UK Ltd.   Ian Serraillier, 'Locking Up' and 'Promotion', both © 1990 Ian Serraillier. Reprinted by permission of the author.   Norman Silver, 'Horrors', © 1990 Norman Silver. Reprinted by permission of the author.   Charles Thomson, 'The Ghoul', 'The Television Ghost' and 'The Trainee Witch', all © 1990 Charles Thomson. Reprinted by permission of the author.   Charles Thomson & Marian Swinger, 'The Vampire's Wedding' and 'A "Humerus" Tale', both © 1990 Charles Thomson and Marian Swinger. Reprinted by permission of the authors.   Dave Ward, 'Candy and the Video' and 'Candy's Camera', both © 1990 Dave Ward. Reprinted by permission of the author.   Clive Webster, 'A Night at the Theatre', 'Lies Again', 'Innocence' and 'Winnie The . . . .', all © 1990 Clive Webster. Reprinted by permission of the author.   Colin West, 'Sir Hector' from *Not To Be Taken Seriously*. Reprinted by permission of Century Hutchinson Ltd. 'Small Ads', © 1990 Colin West. Reprinted by permission of the author.   Raymond Wilson, 'The Haunting', © 1990 Raymond Wilson, and 'Two's Company'. Both reprinted by permission of the author.